To personalize this book, place your own photo here.

For:

From:

Thy love is such I can no way repay;
The heavens reward thee manifold, I pray.

ANNE BRADSTREET

Blessings of a Mother's Love
Copyright 1999 by Zondervan Publishing House

ISBN 0-310-97822-X

Requests for information should be addressed to:
Zondervan Publishing House
Mail Drop B20
Grand Rapids, Michigan 49530
http://www.zondervan.com

Senior Editor: Gwen Ellis
Project Editor: Pat Matuszak
Jacket & Interior Design: Steve Diggs & Friends, Nashville, Tennessee
Cover & Interior Illustrations: Leslie Wu
Interior Photos: Superstock, Inc., The Stock Market & Photodisc Inc.

Printed in China

99 00 01 02/ HK / 4 3 2 1

BLESSINGS OF A

Mother's Love

BLESSINGS OF A

Mother's Love

Celebrating the Gift of Your Faithfulness and Care

ZondervanGifts

We have a gift for inspiration™

What are the blessings of a mother's love?

Her heart is a well of goodwill that nourishes her

children with love and understanding.

Behind every act is an underlying passion to see

her little ones happy and healthy,

thriving in the light of her guidance and faith.

No gold or jeweled gift can crown a mother's life

like a simple word of gratitude

from her beloved child.

"Many women do noble things, but you surpass them all."

Proverbs 31:29

I AM BLESSED

because you gave me life.

Yours were the first eyes that met mine.
Yours the first hand my finger touched. Your smile welcomed me
into this world and is still the most important
one that dawns upon my life.

I prayed for this child, and the LORD has granted me what I asked of him.

1 Samuel 1:27

O LORD; I sing for joy at the works of your hands.

Psalm 92:4

The LORD has made everything beautiful in its time.

Ecclesiastes 3:11

Mother's arms under you,

Her eyes above you.

Sing it high, sing it low,

Love me—I love you.

CHRISTINA ROSSETTI

By wisdom a house is built, and . . . its rooms are
filled with rare and beautiful treasures.

Proverbs 24:3-4

Something wondrous happens when a woman becomes a
mom . . . . suddenly she begins to look at all of life a bit differently.

CAROL KUYKENDALL

May your father and mother be glad;
may she who gave you birth rejoice!

Proverbs 23:25

The LORD created my inmost being;
knit me together in my mother's womb.

Psalm 139:13

I reclined on my hospital bed with my two-day-old
daughter cuddled on my chest. As she slept I caressed her tiny fingers
and wondered how she would use them as she grew up.

MARTHA MANIKAS-FOSTER

*T*hy mother shakes the dreamland tree,
Down falls a little dream for thee.

Traditional Lullaby

*W*hen you lie down, you will not be afraid;
. . . your sleep will be sweet.

Proverbs 3:24

*T*hey say that man is mighty,
He governs land and sea,
He wields a mighty scepter
O'er lesser powers that be;
But a mightier power and stronger
Man from his throne has hurled,
For the hand that rocks the cradle
Is the hand that rules the world.

WILLIAM ROSS WALLACE

May the LORD *make you increase,*
both you and your children.
May you be blessed by the LORD,
the Maker of heaven and earth.

Psalm 115:14-15

*C*ourage

It is in the small things we see it.
The child's first step,
as awesome as an earthquake.

ANNE SEXTON

Adam named his wife Eve, because she would become
the mother of all the living.

Genesis 3:20

We entered motherhood so eagerly—babes in our arms
and stars in our eyes.
So cuddly and cute, these wee ones
took hold of our hearts and lives.

DIANE HEAD

How many are your works, O LORD!
In wisdom you made them all; the earth is full of your creatures.

Psalm 104:24

In the morning I will sing of your love; . . .
you, O God, are my fortress, my loving God.

Psalm 59:16-17

Which one of us hasn't looked on a newborn baby
with amazement and wondered at the exquisite delicacy
of each limb, facial feature, fingernail or eyelash?
Especially if that baby is our own.
It is our responsibility and joy to look at those babies
and delight in their perfectly formed tiny hands and feet
and then worship the one who created those parts
with infinite wisdom, care and direction.

CAROL L. BALDWIN

The Lord himself gives all men life and breath.

Acts 17:25

A hundred years from now it will not matter what
my bank account was, the sort of house I lived in,
or the kind of car I drove . . .
but the world may be different because
I was important in the life of a child.

Anonymous

Jesus said, "Let the little children come to me, and do not hinder them,
for the kingdom of heaven belongs to such as these."

Matthew 19:14

Satisfy us in the morning with your unfailing love,
that we may sing for joy and be glad all our days.

Psalm 90:14

When they see among them their children,
the work of my hands, they will keep my name holy. . . .
Those who are wayward in spirit will gain understanding.

Isaiah 29:23–24

Oh, cleaning and scrubbing will wait till tomorrow,
But children grow up, as I've learned to my sorrow.
So quiet down cobwebs.
Dust go to sleep.
I'm rocking my baby. Babies don't keep.

RUTH HULBURT HAMILTON

There is a time for everything,
and a season for every activity under heaven.

Ecclesiastes 3:1

Jesus said to them,
"Whoever welcomes this little child in my name welcomes me. . . .
For he who is least among you all—he is the greatest."

Luke 9:48

I AM *B*LESSED

by all you've done for me.

There is no giver like a mom. She buys herself last year's styles
from the bargain basement so she can afford to get her children the latest
fashion all their friends will be wearing at school. She stays up late and gets up
early to see that all the loose ends are tied up for tomorrow.
She learns to remember what each child is most likely to forget and runs an endless taxi
and delivery service for lost lunches in a car that looks like everyone's closet.
And she just keeps on giving.

Dear children, let us not love with words or tongue but with actions and in truth.

1 John 3:18

We are partners with the Lord in the ongoing care
and development of his universe.
He asks us to do our best, but never alone.
We are standing beside Jesus, joining him in the joy
of participating in work he created us to do.

What does this mean? He is present when you need help.
He is as adept in your laundry room or boardroom as at church.
Because it is his work, he is a remarkable source of wisdom
for any difficult problem you might face.
All you have to do is ask. Because you are his design,
he is your best source of guidance as you choose your tasks.

KATHY PEEL

She gets up while it is still dark; she provides food for her family.

Proverbs 31:15

"Don't ever become so busy that you fail to realize how very happy you are!"
Mother's statement has meant much to me as I have raised our family. Whenever
I have felt overly busy to the point of neglecting the little joys, the expressions
of appreciation, the realization of how happy we are—whenever play with
the children seemed more of a duty than a privilege,
I have thought of Mother's words. They have been a warning beacon
that has changed my attitude toward life and toward what is valuable.

KATHRYN HILLEN

My love for reading was inborn, but my mother did much
to nurture it. She read to me at night and on long car drives.
She never complained about my weekly library visits, and the worst
punishment she once gave me was to forbid my reading for a day!
And of course she read daily from the best book of all—the Bible.

LORI WALBURG

*Y*ou may have tangible wealth untold,
Caskets of jewels and coffers of gold.
Richer than I you can never be—
I had a mother who read to me.

STRICKLAND GILLIAN

*W*hen we were out of high school, my brothers and I
were talking about how our mom read to us
all the time when we were little.
That day we realized that she had instilled in us
such a love for reading that, years later, whether it was the Bible or a novel,
it was her voice we all heard in our thoughts as we read.

CHRISTI MATUSZAK

Pay attention and listen to the sayings of the wise;
apply your heart to what I teach,
for it is pleasing when you keep them in your heart
and have all of them ready on your lips.

Proverbs 22:17-18

It is not what we do but how much love we put into it.

MOTHER TERESA

When the voices of children are heard on the green
And laughing is heard on the hill,
My heart is at rest within my breast
And everything else is still.

"Then come home my children, the sun is gone down
And the dews of night arise;
Come, come, leave off play, and let us away
Till the morning appears in the skies."

WILLIAM BLAKE

When I was a child, my mother used to sing Luther's "Cradle Hymn"
to me in German as a lullaby. I don't remember the German,
but I'll never forget the melody
and the sound of my mother's voice singing it.

BOB HARTIG

*D*ear Lord,
I want this little boy to know how much I love him.
I want him to know how much joy he has brought to my life. . . .
Help him to know how much he is wanted.

Help me to show him how much. By the sparkle of delight in my eyes
when I smile at him. By how quick I am to drop a mother's chores and play with
him. By the unhurried way I read him stories, even stories I've read to him a
hundred times before. Especially those stories, Lord,
because they will create such a vivid memory for him.

Help me to give this boy a happy childhood, filled with late nights
and pillow fights and stories read by flashlight under his covers.
May his mornings be filled with building forts,
his noons with peanut butter sandwiches eaten in a tree house,
and his afternoons with baseball with the neighbor kids.

May his childhood be filled with such happy times, Lord,
that when he looks back on them, twenty, thirty, forty years hence, the memories
will bring a smile to his face and a reassurance to his heart that
he was wanted, and that he was loved.

ROBERT & MARY WELLS
KEN & JUDY GIRE

In heavenly love abiding,
No change my heart shall fear;
And safe is such confiding,
For nothing changes here.

ANNA L. WARING

You held me in your arms when I was a little one.
You helped me with my faltering steps
until I learned to run.
You watched me and you waited when I went off to school.
You insisted that I try things
I didn't always want to do.
You let me go when it was time to be out on my own.
You pray for God to keep me now
so I'm never left alone.

SUSAN C. JOHNSON

I AM BLESSED

by your care.

No one can care for us like she can.
How many times did she sit up with our fevers and our fears,
holding our hands in her wise and loving way, so that we knew everything
would be all right? Her voice saying comforting words was the one
we most trusted, her lullaby the sweetest to our tired ears and spirits.
When Mom believed in us, no discouragement could keep us down.

A mother's love is like a prism through which the many variations of beauty are revealed in our lives.

Follow the way of love.

1 Corinthians 14:1

The greatest gift my mother has given me is the belief that
I can accomplish anything I pursue. Her words of encouragement
have helped me through the most difficult times in my life.
She is my biggest supporter and my best friend.
Her belief in me is my inspiration to try new things,
and she reminds me that success
and failure do determine a person's character.
Her unconditional love is truly a blessing.

CRISTIN CLARK

I love being a mother because my children allow me to lavish them with love.
They don't suppress my gift of love. All I give them, they happily receive and enjoy.
They have blessed me, prayed for me, thanked me, appreciated me,
and of course, I'm then encouraged to give more love.

MARIE CHAPIAN

*W*hat can nestlings do,
In the nightly dew?
Sleep beneath their mother's wing,
Till day breaks anew.

If in field or tree,
There might only be,
Such a warm, soft, sleep place,
Found for me!

CHRISTINA ROSSETTI

Even the sparrow has found a home,
and the swallow a nest for herself,
where she may have her young—
a place near your altar,
O LORD Almighty, my King and my God.
Blessed are those who dwell in your house;
they are ever praising you.

Psalm 84:3-4

There are longings of the heart that seem to be universal—
the desire to find true love, the desire that someone will affirm
our inherent value regardless of our situation,
the hope that we can change.

CONNIE NEAL

One thing I will always remember about my mom
is that whenever I was sick she would sit by my bed
and just gently stroke my hair
to help make me feel better.
It was such a soothing, comforting act of love
that made me feel reassured
and cared for.

PATRICIA MATTHEWS

Round the laps of their mothers,
Many sisters and brothers,
Like birds in their nest,
Are ready for rest.

WILLIAM BLAKE

Children have their different natures.
Those parents are wise that can fit their nurture according to their nature.

ANNE BRADSTREET

My mom not only patiently cared for her four children,
she also adopted every baby bird, stray puppy, kitten, rabbit, turtle,
or other animal that we brought home.
She even gave them all names and talked to them like people.
Our home was always full of fun.

PAT MATUSZAK

Are your children grown?
Yet in your mind they are still your little ones,
so bring those grown men or women to Jesus
as the children you know them to be.
Jesus will touch them and bless them.

ROSALIND RINKER

In him we live and move and have our being.

Acts 17:28

Jesus gave some special parental instructions. "Love and take care
of each other. The way you treat each other will tell the world
about our family, so remember whose child you are."

GLORIA GAITHER

The highest function of my mother love would be fulfilled
when my love was strong enough to cut the apron strings
and let my adult child move off into his own life.
I would succeed as a mother
only when I had so reared my child
that he would no longer have need of me.
Yet this is not tragedy; it is growth.
This is no betrayal of love.
This is love.

CATHERINE MARSHALL

My Boy

I look at the shiny-shaggy hair and round, blue-gray eyes;
the small pink tongue struggling impatiently
against tiny white teeth to form a word,
to convey an exciting newborn thought;
the broad little boy hand-covered with dirt,
reaching to touch my cheek;
and suddenly I realize
the astounding responsibilities that are mine
before that hand expands to a man's hand.

O God, hold my son's hand while he crosses
the danger-filled street to manhood.

Susan L. Lenzkes

My mother was always beautiful and a sharp dresser even for simple outings.
One recollection I have of my mother is of her, with six kids in tow,
speed-shopping at the grocery store. I can still vividly recall the
"click, click, click" of her high heels rapidly walking down the aisle as
I raced to try to keep up with her and throw extra items in the cart.

MARK ELLERMETS

The mother makes up her mind to a certain course of action, which she believes
to be right and best. The children clamor against it and declare it shall not be.
But the mother, knowing that she is mistress and not they, pursues her course
lovingly and calmly in spite of all their clamors; and the result is that the
children are sooner or later won over to the mother's course of action
and fall in with her decision, and all is harmonious and happy.

HANNAH WHITALL SMITH

I AM *Blessed*

by your thoughtfulness.

Mom always understands when no one else can.
She is like the Red Cross for spiritual emergencies. She has the
ability to put herself in anyone's place and know how they would feel.
She comes up with the right words to mend a broken spirit,
the right little card or note to encourage,
and knows when it is time to let well enough alone.

*Whatever you do, whether in word or deed, do it all in the name of the
Lord Jesus, giving thanks to God the Father through him.*

Colossians 3:17

I'm forty-two years old, but my mom still blesses my life. I am very busy these
days with a new job, four children, and many community commitments.
Last Christmas I had a perfect gift in mind for my husband but didn't know where
to look and had no time to shop. My mom, who has a good eye for quality and
value, scoured the shops in her town, found just what I wanted,
and delivered it to my home. She even included gift wrap!

LINDA WACYK

We are rich because, as the highest of God's creation,
he gave us the ability to love back, to return the affection.
It is almost as great to be able to love back
as it is to know you are loved.

GLORIA GAITHER

Keep on loving each other.

Hebrews 13:1

For Mercy has a human heart,
Pity, a human face,
And Love, the human form divine,
And Peace, the human dress.

WILLIAM BLAKE

She opens her arms to the poor
and extends her hands to the needy.

Proverbs 31:20

Speak up for those who cannot speak for themselves.

Proverbs 31:8

Driving on the highway, I am often confronted by the automobile
bumper sticker with the high-flown injunction
"Practice senseless acts of beauty and random acts of kindness."
Appealing as it sounds, this is not quite a Christian ideal, because it
presupposes a meaningless, random universe without a God of grace,
a bitter world that needs to be sweetened,
transformed by a kind of magic wand of human goodwill.
If one does not believe in God, all acts become, in a way, senseless, purposeless.
All of us would agree that random kindness and beauty are to be preferred to
random violence and aggression, but rather than acting senselessly
and randomly, let us, in response to God's grace in our own lives,
commit purposeful kindness in his name and perform, deliberately,
actions of unstinting compassion and generosity
that will reflect God's loving nature, vibrantly alive in us.

LUCI SHAW

*We are God's workmanship, created in Christ Jesus
to do good works, which God prepared in advance for us to do.*

Ephesians 2:10

When you love someone,
you naturally want to do things
for them that will bring them pleasure.
Preparing a favorite meal, or surprising someone
with a fresh bouquet of fragrant flowers, are ways
we express love from one person to another.
Similarly, God loves us so much that he has given us
thousands of flavors to enjoy,
and gardens of colorful, scented flowers
to bring us pleasure.

TERRY WILLITS

A word aptly spoken
is like apples of gold in settings of silver.

Proverbs 25:11

Blessed is the influence of one true, loving human soul on another.

GEORGE ELIOT

Do not forget to entertain strangers, for by so doing
some people have entertained angels without knowing it.

Hebrews 13:2

They are always generous and lend freely;
their children will be blessed.

Psalm 37:26

We are our children's last, best hope. We are there.
We put dinner on the table, clothes in their drawers.
Life goes on, perhaps tentatively, maybe in tears . . . but we will survive.
That is a tremendous, vital reassurance for our children.

And just because we are there, day in and day out,
we may throw the balance toward their lifetime stability.

KATE CONVISSOR

Each one should use whatever gift he has received to serve others,
faithfully administering God's grace in its various forms.
If anyone speaks, he should do it as one speaking the very words of God.
If anyone serves, he should do it with the strength God provides,
so that in all things God may be praised through Jesus Christ.

1 Peter 4:10-11

A heart open to God, with room prepared for the guest of
the Holy Spirit, which welcomes the presence of Christ.
This is what we share with those to whom we open our doors.

My three-dollar oak table has become an altar
where hungry hearts have been nourished with the bread of life.
Our living room has been made a sanctuary
where sacraments of comfort and communion have been offered,
where we have shared in the fellowship
of human suffering and human delight.

KAREN BURTON MAINS

I AM *B*LESSED
by your example.

Like a conductor with a baton, a mother sets the tone and tempo for her home.
If she is in a hurry, the whole household seems to rush around like bees.
If she is singing, everyone begins to hum and can't get her melody out of their heads.
The lessons her children learn by just watching her life from the background
will become examples that turn into the standards
by which they evaluate their own lives.

A cheerful heart is good medicine.

Proverbs 17:22

Ruth Graham boasts of a sign in her kitchen that reads,
"Divine service conducted here three times daily."
When everything becomes a token of God's love,
you feel as though you possess everything.
Our duties are sweet when seen as service to God.

JONI EARECKSON TADA

*The LORD has done great things for us,
and we are filled with joy.*

Psalm 126:3

*W*e all have imperfections. We live in an imperfect world.
Our created purpose is to let God's light shine through every facet of our being,
expressing his colors and beauty through us in ways no one else can.

If you look at a ring under the microscope every day
and become intimately familiar with every flaw,
you might be embarrassed by it.
But that is not how God meant the beauty of diamonds to be seen.
The beauty of a diamond is seen when someone holds it up in
the sunlight and everyone can see it sparkle.

We are created to shine with the light of God's creative genius.
When you appreciate yourself in all your uniqueness,
you will dare to hold your life up to the light.
You will dare to live out the beauty you were created to express . . .
cleaned and polished with the forgiveness of God.

CONNIE NEAL

My mom has always taught us:
"Do not worry about how someone treats you,
but just worry about how you respond! You will be judged accordingly."

This goes along with the Scripture that says
to do to others as you would have them do to you.

VICTORIA HARRIS

My mother taught me underneath a tree,
And sitting down before the heat of day,
She took me on her lap and kissed me,
And pointing to the east, began to say:

"Look on the rising sun: there God does live
And give his light, and gives his heat away;
And flowers and trees and beasts and men receive
Comfort in the morning, joy in the noon day."

WILLIAM BLAKE

I have no greater joy than to hear that my children are walking in the truth.

3 John 4

*If your heart is wise,
then my heart will be glad;
my inmost being will rejoice
when your lips speak what is right.*

Proverbs 23:15-16

My prayer will continue to be that no matter what profession
my daughter chooses, at the core she will truly succeed by
being a righteous and godly woman, full of
"faith, love, endurance and gentleness."

Martha Manikas-Foster

Do to others as you would have them do to you.

Luke 6:31

The mother's heart is the child's schoolroom.

HENRY WARD BEECHER

Be shepherds of God's flock that is under your care, serving as overseers—not because you must, but because you are willing, as God wants you to be . . . not lording it over those entrusted to you, but being examples to the flock.

1 Peter 5:2–3

Every woman takes the threads and materials each day hands her and works them into the tapestry that becomes her life.

NANCY CORBETT COLE

*Teach the older women to be reverent in the way they live,
not to be slanderers or addicted to much wine, but to teach what is good.
Then they can train the younger women to love their husbands and children,
to be self-controlled and pure, to be busy at home, to be kind, and to be subject
to their husbands, so that no one will malign the word of God.*

TITUS 2:3-5

Ever since I was young, I have watched my mother's example,
and I have learned much about waiting and building.
Her life has been one of much waiting and much giving.
She built a place of shelter—her ark—virtually alone,
with Daddy away so much of the time.
The waiting periods were often long and quite difficult.

When she had nothing left to give, she went to the source of her strength
and the supplier of all her needs and was unexplainably replenished.
So much so, that we children never saw or knew of her needs.
She gave us the sunshine, and gave Jesus all the rest.

GIGI GRAHAM TCHIVIDJIAN

An honest answer is like a kiss on the lips.

Proverbs 24:26

A while back I saw a bumper sticker that read,
"Life is short. Eat dessert first."
Though pigging out on dessert isn't wise dieting advice, I liked the slogan.
To me it said, "Lighten up." Homes will not break up,
children will not go to bed hungry, and the sun will not fall from the sky
if I miss double-coupon day or fail to get my thighs in shape.
We've got to keep in touch with reality.
God wants us to be obedient, not obsessive.
Living simply means concentrating on what's important
in light of eternity, and not taking the rest of life too seriously.

ANNIE CHAPMAN

She speaks with wisdom,
and faithful instruction is on her tongue.

Proverbs 31:26

My mother's mother, my Granny, more or less raised me.
She was straight out of Appalachia in South Carolina with no "readin'
or writin'" skills. Her greatest knowledge came from many "sayings"
that she was very fond of repeating to anyone who was in
hearing distance, but especially me.

Two she mentioned often to me were (I can hear her still):
"Sis, if you want a taste of Heaven's joys,
think more of the Lord and less of the boys";
and "Lipstick, perfume, powder, and paint
make a little plain girl look like what she ain't."

Others were, "Don't try to stir someone else's pot
when you can't keep your own from scorching,"
and "Talk about me all you please. I'll talk about you on my knees."
Granny was eighty-six marvelous years old when she joined my
grandfather in the best home they ever had.

SANDRA SMITH

*M*y mother was the most beautiful woman I ever saw.
All I am I owe to my mother.
I attribute all my success in life to the moral, intellectual
and physical education I received from her.

GEORGE WASHINGTON

"Lift up your eyes and look around;
all your sons gather and come to you.
As surely as I live," declares the LORD,
"you will wear them all as ornaments;
you will put them on,
like a bride."

Isaiah 49:18

It is not possible to always be happy. It *is* possible to always have the joy of the Lord. Some have described it as a calm centeredness that tickles at the edges. It's a solid assurance that laughs if given the chance. It is unwavering confidence that can't help but look on the bright side.

JONI EARECKSON TADA

The Lord delights in those who put their hope in his unfailing love.

Psalm 147:11

Mothers keep family and friends close to our hearts and prayers. They are the ones who remember—the keepers of the true riches of family—the favorite stories, characters, and songs that give birth to our family history and make it unique to one special group of people out of all others in the world.

PAT MATUSZAK

I AM *BLESSED*

by your faithfulness.

A mother's loyalty can be counted on to such an extent
that children sometimes don't even want to ask her opinion—
"Of course you think it's great, You're my mom." But that same steadfast presence
is the one they seek when life gets uncertain and stormy situations arise.
Mom's safe harbor is one they can count on as an anchoring place in this world.

If we love one another, God lives in us and his love is made complete in us.

1 John 4:12

*M*other's wise words,
Her heart kind and warm,
A love I can count on
In every storm.

Love, faithful love,
recalled thee to my mind—
But how could I forget thee?
Through what power,
Even for the least division of an hour!

WILLIAM WORDSWORTH

Can a mother forget the baby at her breast, . . . the child she has borne?
See, I have engraved you on the palms of my hands;
your walls are ever before me.

Isaiah 49:15-16

If I speak in the tongues of men and of angels, but have not love,
I am only a resounding gong or a clanging cymbal.

1 Corinthians 13:1

I want my children to know the values I hold most dear,
which do not change no matter the times;
that they are in my thoughts and prayers often every day;
and that each occupies a very special room in my heart
and owns love that is his alone and that can never be occupied
by another or taken away by anything he can ever say or do.

MARIAN WRIGHT EDELMAN

*N*ever, bright flame, may be denied to me
Thy dear life, imaging close sympathy.

ELLEN STURGIS HOOPER

The LORD *looks at the heart.*

1 Samuel 16:7

Faith delivers us from the temptation to believe
that events are random—that life is meaningless.
Faith doesn't provide answers; it stands silently—pointing.
It whispers rather than shouts, draws instead of pushing.

KATE CONVISSOR

Faith is being sure of what we hope for and certain of what we do not see.

Hebrews 11:1

We shouldn't deny the pain of what happens in our lives.
We should just refuse to focus only on the valleys.

CHARLES SWINDOLL

There I will give her back her vineyards,
and will make the Valley of Achor a door of hope.
There she will sing as in the days of her youth.

Hosea 2:15

We say with confidence, "The Lord is my helper; I will not be afraid."

Hebrews 13:6

The Christian mother must turn a deaf ear to the babble of voices
vying for her attention and listen to God.
It is in Scripture that she will find the only
safe and reliable information about how to fulfill
her calling as a wife and mother.

BARBARA BUSH

*Blessed are those whose strength is in the LORD,
who have set their hearts on pilgrimage.*

Psalm 84:5

What a lioness was your mother
among the lions!
She lay down among the young lions
and reared her cubs. . . .

Your mother was like a vine in your vineyard
planted by the water;
it was fruitful and full of branches
because of abundant water.

Ezekiel 19:2, 10

A bountiful garden—and a life open and receptive
to friendship—both are sanctuaries for all seasons.
The sum of them brings to our lives a glorious mélange of
color, texture, and form at once reminding us of our roots,
enriching our present, and giving purpose to our future.

SUE BUCHANAN

He who sows courtesy reaps friendship,
and he who plants kindness gathers love.

BASIL

Diamonds pale and fortunes fade when compared to a child
who's on his way to making a positive contribution to humanity.

VALERIE BELL

Low at his feet lay thy burden of carefulness,
High on his heart he will bear it for thee,
Comfort thy sorrows, and answer thy prayerfulness,
Guiding thy steps as may best for thee be.

WILLIAM F. SHERWIN

Sweet are the thoughts that savor of content,
The quiet mind is richer than a crown.

ROBERT GREENE

My mom always remembers to forgive my mistakes—
and forgets to be offended!

The heart of a mother is a deep abyss at the bottom of which
you will always find forgiveness.

HONORÉ DE BALZAC

*Forgive whatever grievances you may have against one another.
Forgive as the Lord forgave you. And over all these virtues put on love,
which binds them all together in perfect unity.*

Colossians 3:13–14

Into any ordinary day, the grace of a mother's love
may break through with unexpected gifts as bright as any rainbow.

PAT MATUSZAK

Ask the primary question: "What does my child need?"
The answer is not necessarily clean pillowcases,
vegetables, and proper bedtimes.
The answer is: Our children need us to be the guardians
of the trust, the protectors of family relationships,
parents with clear focus and pure hearts.
They need us to have faithful hearts—to
care deeply, passionately, and affectionately for them.

VALERIE BELL

It seems to me that everyone, simply, wants to be loved.
So it is love that transforms the abandoned child
into a new citizen of the forgiving world,
the mother world,
the universal embrace.

CHRISTOPHER DE VINCK

One day in the mountain region of Scotland, a gigantic eagle
snatched a little baby out of his crib and flew away with him.
The people of the village ran out after the big bird, but the eagle perched
itself upon a nearby mountain crag. Could the child possibly be rescued?
A sailor tried to climb the ascent, but he was at last obliged to give up the attempt.
A robust Highlander, accustomed to climbing those mountains,
tried next and even his strength failed. At last a poor peasant woman came forward.
She put her feet upon one shelf on the rock, then on the second,
then on the third, and in this manner she rose to the very top of the cliff. While all
below held their breath for sheer fright,
she came down step by step until she stood at the bottom of the rock
with the child safely in her arms. Immediately shouts of praise arose
from the crowd that had gathered.

Why did that woman succeed when the strong sailor and the
experienced mountain climber had failed?
Because that woman was the mother of the baby.
Her love for her baby had given her the courage to do
what the others had failed to do.

HENRIETTA MEARS

Now Elimelech, Naomi's husband, died, and she was left with her two sons. They married Moabite women, one named Orpah and the other Ruth. After they had lived there about ten years, both Mahlon and Kilion also died, and Naomi was left without her two sons and her husband. . . .

But Naomi said, "Return home, my daughters. Why would you come with me? Am I going to have any more sons, who could become your husbands? Return home, my daughters; I am too old to have another husband. Even if I thought there was still hope for me—even if I had a husband tonight and then gave birth to sons—would you wait until they grew up? Would you remain unmarried for them? No, my daughters. It is more bitter for me than for you, because the LORD's hand has gone out against me!"

At this they wept again. Then Orpah kissed her mother-in-law good-by, but Ruth clung to her. "Look," said Naomi, "your sister-in-law is going back to her people and her gods. Go back with her."

But Ruth replied, "Don't urge me to leave you or to turn back from you. Where you go I will go, and where you stay I will stay. Your people will be my people and your God my God. Where you die I will die, and there I will be buried. May the LORD deal with me, be it ever so severely, if anything but death separates you and me."

Ruth 1:3-5, 11-17

I AM BLESSED

because you are my friend.

One of the most significant crossings in life is when mother
and child grow up into friends. She looks at her child with new eyes
and sees a person ready to bear the reality friendship brings—ready to see
Mom as a real person with some knots in her fabric instead of that seamless
motherly image. Ready to be depended upon instead of needing to be dependent.
She finds a companion who can understand instead of only needing to be understood.
It is the final tribute to their relationship to be able to say, "We are friends."

Give her the reward she has earned.

Proverbs 31:31

I heard songwriter and author Gloria Gaither say once, speaking to a group of women, that a mother's primary goal should be to work herself out of a job. That's hard to accept, because it means gradually making yourself physically, although not emotionally, dispensable to your child. But it's the only way to raise capable, responsible, emotionally healthy children.

KAREN HULL

There is a time for everything, and a season for every activity under heaven.

Ecclesiastes 3:1

We learn to recognize the seeds of friendship from those modeled by our parents and other adults from our childhood experiences.

GLORIA GAITHER

My mom is a real friend—the kind who believes
in the real me, even when I doubt myself.

Oh the comfort of feeling safe with a person.
Having neither to weigh words nor measure thoughts but
pouring them all out like chaff and grain together.

GEORGE ELIOT

If my mom calls me just to say hello,
I know she won't give up if the line is busy.

ELEANOR JONES

*If one falls down,
his friend can help him up.
But pity the man who falls
and has no one to help him up!*

Ecclesiastes 4:10

Friendship is a sheltering tree.

SAMUEL TAYLOR COLERIDGE

A friend is someone who can see through you and still enjoys the show.

The Farmer's Almanac

Be devoted to one another.... Honor one another above yourselves.

Romans 12:10

My mom loves me for who I am,
but tells me the truth when I need to hear it.

PATRICIA BELL

Wounds from a friend can be trusted.

Proverbs 27:6

Friendship that flows from the heart cannot be frozen by adversity,
as the water that flows from the spring cannot congeal in winter.

JAMES FENIMORE COOPER

Remember me when far away;
Embrace me when I'm near.
You're a friend I cherish,
Forever and sincere.

Author Unknown

My first friend was my mother. She taught me my first lessons about friendship
by being my first, last, and most enduring friend, and even though she is gone from
this earth, she is far from gone from my life.

GLORIA GAITHER

Loving and being loved—being connected, valued, befriended,
cherished by another—is a compelling need that permeates
the life of every human being on God's earth.

JOY MACKENZIE

Friends and family are one treasure from this life that we may keep in the next.

IS THIS ALL?

If life has no more purpose
Than to fight to keep alive,
If all there is to living
Is to struggle and to strive
Without a contribution
To some worthwhile total plan,
God went to too much trouble
Just to fashion man.

GLORIA GAITHER'S MOTHER

My mother was quite a pianist and enjoyed getting us around
the piano for family sing-a-longs. I always felt she liked to hear me sing the best,
because she would actually stop the others and make them be quiet so that she
could hear me! (One of my sisters, who happens to have a very lovely
voice, still complains about being "so offended" at that time—
but I think she's dealt with it now!)

MARK ELLERMETS

When my daughter Tiffany was four weeks old, we flew home
to be with my parents. As I deplaned, holding my baby,
I immediately spotted my mother. Her dark eyes brimmed
with joy, and we hugged, laughing and weeping.
Now as I placed Tiffany in her arms, I knew I had finally returned
some of that joy to her, just as I had always dreamed of doing.
That was the best week I've ever spent with my mother—
a precious gift of time from God.

JAN DRAVECKY

I AM *B*LESSED

because you pray.

One great strength of a mother is not that
she possesses all the answers to meet everyone's need;
it's being willing to admit she cannot do it all herself.
Her ability to look outside herself, and her wisdom
to find the answers in God, are an eternal flame to give her family
the spiritual help so vital to its survival.

*M*y mom has made a real difference in my life,
without choosing my path for me.

LINDA LEY

Let the word of Christ dwell in you richly
as you teach and admonish one another with all wisdom,
and as you sing psalms, hymns and spiritual songs
with gratitude in your hearts to God.

Colossians 3:16

*M*y mother's love, a precious gift, sent from heaven above.
Her prayer for me is Mom's amen
to God's own gift of love.

Author Unknown

It is with your heart that you believe.

Romans 10:10

*P*rayer enlarges the heart until it is capable of containing
God's gift of himself. Ask and seek, and your heart
will grow big enough to receive him and to keep him as your own.

MOTHER TERESA

I have never forgotten when I was about five or six,
my mother told me that God is always with me and knows what I do
and what I need. This has always made me feel safe and secure—
and always made me think twice before trying to get away with anything!

CONNIE KOEHLER THOMPSON

Let the peace of Christ rule in your hearts.

Colossians 3:15

A mother's heart loves you as you are, and as you dream to become.
Youth fades; love droops, the leaves of friendship fall;
A mother's secret hope outlives them all.

OLIVER WENDELL HOLMES

Seeds are the symbolic heart . . . unassuming, even drab,
indistinct contents of paper packet.
Little hopes that are waiting to be nurtured to full bloom.

GLORIA GAITHER

I remember my mother's prayers and they have always followed me.
They have clung to me all my life.

ABRAHAM LINCOLN

*I*t is the earnest prayer of one who believes that leads to answers.

CHARLES H. SPURGEON

*O*n my knees beside the bathtub as I bathed my little son,
I thought how I still struggle with the problem
of controlling my mind and my tongue.
That afternoon as I knelt to scrub that sturdy little body,
the tub became my altar; the bathroom, my temple.
I bowed my head, covered my face.
I asked the Lord to forgive me and to give me more and more
the mind and heart and attitude of Christ.

GIGI GRAHAM TCHIVIDJIAN

*T*hrough all the heav'ns what beauteous dyes are spread!
But the west glories in the deepest red;
So may our breasts with ev'ry virtue glow,
The living temples of our God below!

PHILLIS WHEATLEY

The hour I spend with the Lord is always the best part of my day.
I turn the lawn chair to face the sun and settle in.
This is my personal "Psalm 23" setting.
Usually so busy, here I allow myself to slow down, reflect, quiet my heart,
pour out my soul, and listen to God.

BECKY TIRABASSI

We cannot go with our children into adulthood;
they will have to conquer their own ground, as we did.
But we can keep the home fires burning and the welcome mat out,
sensitive to the signals we receive from their battleground
and ready for a time when our young adult needs a temporary "R and R"
or a chance to fall back and regroup.
"Having done everything," we can only cover them in the armor
of our prayers as they go forward.

CAROLYN JOHNSON

Our deep need to be assured that someone really understands us,
to share our innermost feelings with another, is not silly.
It is a yearning built into our natures by God at creation.
It is essential, then, for us to know that we are not on our own
as mothers without a divine hand to guide
or a source of wisdom to which to turn.
The God who understands each of us completely
as a person is also our everlasting Father
and the Master of every skill needed for godly motherhood.

BARBARA BUSH

I AM BLESSED

by a rich heritage.

Mothers have mentors, too. From Bible heroines like Sarah
to modern-day leaders and their own mothers, women of faith
seek guidance of those who have laid godly foundations in their homes.
In modeling their lives after solid Christians,
moms give their own children a birthright of faith.

Susanna Wesley, Corrie ten Boom, Catherine Booth, Florence Nightingale.
These women changed the world. Their stories moved me to want to do
the same. But they also gave me another gift: they showed me the
secrets of how such influence grows.
From them I learned that the ripple effect happens
over the course of a lifetime. And the real magnitude of our impact
may not be felt until after we've died.
Faithfully serving wherever God planted them was the key to these women's lives.
We serve with joy wherever he chooses,
and he causes the ripples from our service to spread to the world.

ANNIE CHAPMAN

I know that what we write on the heart of a child
cannot be erased and when a mother is at home
to contribute to the indelible marks
that are written on a child's tender heart,
it is a rich heritage.

BARBARA JOHNSON

May you live to see your children's children.

Psalm 128:6

One of the blessings of faith in Christ is that
we recognize that raising our kids isn't all up to us.
We need the security of knowing Christ
and of being able to spend time with him on a
regular basis, praying and reading his Word.
His principles are timeless.
They alone last through all social changes.
They are applicable in every situation.
And they provide us with a foundation
upon which to raise our families.
A vital relationship with Christ is like the
rudder of the ship that keeps individuals
and families on course
no matter what the weather.

SUSAN ALEXANDER YATES

The LORD *appeared to us in the past, saying:*
"I have loved you with an everlasting love;
I have drawn you with loving-kindness."

Jeremiah 31:3

We who are willing to be used also impart a legacy of Christ's love
in the lives of those we encounter.
As the old saying goes,
"You may be the only Bible someone ever reads."

MARY PIELENZ HAMPTON

You are a letter from Christ . . . written not with ink
but with the Spirit of the living God,
not on tablets of stone
but on tablets of human hearts.

2 Corinthians 3:3

Only love can be divided endlessly and still not diminish.

ANNE MORROW LINDBERGH

We continually remember before our God and Father
your work produced by faith, your labor prompted by love,
and your endurance inspired by hope
in our Lord Jesus Christ.

1 Thessalonians 1:3

The warming hearth of a mother's love is built just one brick at a time.

SUZANNE JACOBS

Christ's love compels us.

2 Corinthians 5:14

Knowing that God accepts us simply because we are his gives us security.
Understanding that there is total acceptance of us
by our families because we are family
will create an atmosphere of approval and a sense of family identity.

A home whose atmosphere is marked by the ingredient of love
will be a home where the members sense acceptance from one another,
a home where they return to be filled up to go out into the world.

SUSAN ALEXANDER YATES

I have been reminded of your [Timothy's] sincere faith,
which first lived in your grandmother Lois and in your mother Eunice
and, I am persuaded, now lives in you also.

2 Timothy 1:5

She watches over the affairs of her household
and does not eat the bread of idleness.
Her children arise and call her blessed;
her husband also, and he praises her:
"Many women do noble things,
but you surpass them all."
Charm is deceptive, and beauty is fleeting;
but a woman who fears the LORD *is to be praised.*
Give her the reward she has earned,
and let her works bring her praise at the city gate.

Proverbs 31:27–31

The courage that my mother had
Went with her, and is with her still:
Rock from New England quarried.

EDNA ST. VINCENT MILLAY

As from my window at the first glimpse of dawn
I watch the rising mist that heralds day,
And see by God's strong hand the curtain drawn
That through the night has hid the world away.

ALICE MACDONALD KIPLING

Alice Macdonald Kipling was the mother of the famed poet Rudyard Kipling.
According to her son, she was not only "the wittiest woman in India" but a poet as well.

Jesus went to a town called Nain, and his disciples and a large crowd went along
with him. As he approached the town gate, a dead person was being
carried out—the only son of his mother, and she was a widow.
And a large crowd from the town was with her.
When the Lord saw her, his heart went out to her and he said, "Don't cry."

Then he went up and touched the coffin, and those carrying it stood still.
He said, "Young man, I say to you, get up!"
The dead man sat up and began to talk, and Jesus gave him back to his mother.

They were all filled with awe and praised God.

Luke 7:11–16

The LORD *appeared to Abraham near the great trees of Mamre*
while he was sitting at the entrance to his tent in the heat of the day.
Abraham looked up and saw three men standing nearby.
When he saw them, he hurried from the entrance of his tent
to meet them and bowed low to the ground.

He said, "If I have found favor in your eyes,
my lord, do not pass your servant by.
Let a little water be brought, and then you may all wash your feet
and rest under this tree.
Let me get you something to eat, so you can be refreshed
and then go on your way—now that you have come to your servant."

"Very well," they answered, "do as you say."

So Abraham hurried into the tent to Sarah. "Quick," he said,
"get three seahs of fine flour and knead it and bake some bread."...

While they ate, he stood near them under a tree.

"Where is your wife Sarah?" they asked him.

"There, in the tent," he said.

Then the LORD said, "I will surely return to you about this time next year,
and Sarah your wife will have a son."

Now Sarah was listening at the entrance to the tent, which was behind him.
Abraham and Sarah were already old and well advanced in years,
and Sarah was past the age of childbearing.
So Sarah laughed to herself as she thought,
"After I am worn out and my master is old, will I now have this pleasure?"

Then the LORD said to Abraham, "Why did Sarah laugh and say,'
Will I really have a child, now that I am old?'
Is anything too hard for the LORD?
I will return to you at the appointed time next year
and Sarah will have a son."

Sarah was afraid, so she lied and said, "I did not laugh."

But he said, "Yes, you did laugh." . . .

Now the LORD was gracious to Sarah as he had said,
and the LORD did for Sarah what he had promised.
Sarah became pregnant and bore a son to Abraham in his old age,
at the very time God had promised him.

Abraham gave the name Isaac to the son Sarah bore him. . . .

Sarah said, "God has brought me laughter,
and everyone who hears about this will laugh with me."
And she added, "Who would have said to Abraham that
Sarah would nurse children?
Yet I have borne him a son in his old age."

Genesis 18:1-15; 21:1-7

SOURCES

Thank you to those who contributed personal letters to this collection.

Cristin Clark, Mark Ellermets, Bob Hartig, Susan Johnson, Christi Matuszak, Patricia Matthews, Sandra Smith, Lori Walburg, Carol L. Baldwin, Martha Manikas-Foster, Gloria Gaither, Diane Head, Alice Macdonald Kipling, Karen Burton Mains, Connie Neal, Rosalind Rinker, Gigi Graham Tchividjian, Anna Waring, *NIV Women's Devotional Bible* (Grand Rapids: Zondervan Publishing House, 1993).

Valerie Bell, *Getting Out of Your Kids' Faces & Into Their Hearts* (Grand Rapids: Zondervan Publishing House, 1994).

Valerie Bell, *Nobody's Children* (Dallas: Word Publishing, 1989).

Barbara Bush, *Mastering Motherhood* (Grand Rapids: Zondervan Publishing House, 1991).

Marie Chapian, *To Love and Be Loved* (Grand Rapids: Fleming H. Revell, 1983).

Annie Chapman with Maureen Rank, *Smart Women Keep It Simple* (Minneapolis: Bethany House Publishers, 1992).

Nancy Corbett Cole, *Tapestry of Life, Book 2* (Tulsa: Honor Books, 1995).

Kate Convissor, *Young Widow* (Grand Rapids: Zondervan Publishing House, 1992).

Eleanor I. Doan, compiler, *431 Quotes from the Notes of Henrietta Mears* (Ventura, Calif.: Gospel Light Publications, 1970).

Jan Dravecky, *A Joy I'd Never Known* (Grand Rapids: Zondervan Publishing House, 1976).

Marian Wright Edelman, *The Measure of Our Success* (Boston: Beacon Press, 1992).

Jean Fleming, *A Mother's Heart* (Colorado Springs: NavPress, 1996).

Ruth Hulburt Hamilton, *Ladies Home Journal* (October 1958).

Kathryn Hillen, *Memories* (Grand Rapids: Zondervan Publishing House, 1987).

Karen Hull, *The Mommy Book* (Grand Rapids: Zondervan Publishing House, 1986).

Brenda Hunter, *Home by Choice* (Sisters, Ore.: Multnomah Publishing, 1991).

Beth Jameson, *Hold Me Tight* (Old Tappan, N.J.: Fleming H. Revell, 1980).

Barbara Johnson in *Mommy Where Are You?* by Kathi Mills (Eugene, Ore.: Harvest House Publishers, 1992).

Carolyn Johnson, *Forever a Parent* (Grand Rapids: Zondervan Publishing House, 1992).

Carol Kuykendall, *A Mother's Footprints of Faith* (Grand Rapids: Zondervan Publishing House, 1997).

Anne Morrow Lindbergh, *Gift from the Sea* (New York: Pantheon Books, 1955).

Catherine Marshall, *To Live Again* (Charlotte, N.C.: Commission Press, 1957).

Carole Mayhall, *When God Whispers* (Colorado Springs: NavPress, 1994).

Robin Rice Morris, "Heroes" from *Mothers at Home* homepage, www.mah.org.

Connie Neal, *Dancing in the Arms of God* (Grand Rapids: Zondervan Publishing House, 1995).

Donna Otto, *The Stay at Home Mom* (Eugene, Ore.: Harvest House Publishers, 1991).

Kathy Peel, *Do Plastic Surgeons Take VISA?* (Dallas: Word Publishing, 1992).

Anne Wilson Schaef, *Meditations for Women Who Do Too Much* (San Francisco: Harper & Row, 1990).

Luci Shaw, *Water My Soul* (Grand Rapids: Zondervan Publishing House, 1998).

Hannah Whitall Smith, *The Christian's Secret of a Happy Life* (Old Tappan, N.J.: Fleming H. Revell, 1942).

Margaret B. Spiess, *Gather Me Together, Lord* (Grand Rapids, Baker Book House, 1982).

Dr. Stephan & Gigi Tchividjian, *Our Search for Serenity* (Minneapolis: World Wide, 1981).

Becky Tirabassi, *Wild Things Happen When I Pray* (Grand Rapids: Zondervan Publishing House, 1993).

Robert G. Wells, M.D., Ken Gire, Mary C. Wells, Judy Gire, *Miracle of Life* (Grand Rapids: Zondervan Publishing House, 1993).

Susan Alexander Yates, *And Then I Had Kids* (Brentwood, Tenn.: Wolgemuth & Hyatt Publishers, 1988).

William Ross Wallace.

Strickland Gillian, 1869-1954.

Susan L. Lenzkes, 1981, available through the author.

Joni Eareckson Tada, *God's Precious Love* (Grand Rapids: Zondervan Publishing House, 1998).